JEZ BUTTERWORTH

Mojo (1995), *The Night Heron* (2002), *The Winterling* (2006)
and *Jerusalem* (2009) were all premiered at the Royal Court
Theatre, London. *Parlour Song* was premiered at the Atlantic
Theater, New York, in 2008, and at the Almeida Theatre,
London, in 2009. *Mojo* won the George Devine Award, the
Olivier Award for Best Comedy and the Writers' Guild, Critics'
Circle and Evening Standard Awards for Most Promising
Playwright. Jez directed the film adaptation of *Mojo* (1998)
starring Ian Hart and Harold Pinter, and the film *Birthday
Girl* (2002) starring Nicole Kidman and Ben Chaplin. In 2007
he was awarded the E.M. Forster Award by the American
Academy of Arts and Letters.

Jez Butterworth

PARLOUR SONG

NICK HERN BOOKS
London
www.nickhernbooks.co.uk

A Nick Hern Book

Parlour Song first published in Great Britain as a paperback original in 2009 by Nick Hern Books Limited, 14 Larden Road, London W3 7ST

Parlour Song copyright © 2009 Jez Butterworth

Jez Butterworth has asserted his right to be identified as the author of this work

Cover image: David McGlynn/Photographer's Choice/Getty Images
Cover design: Ned Hoste, 2H

Typeset by Nick Hern Books, London
Printed and bound in Great Britain by CPI Antony Rowe, Chippenham, Wiltshire

A CIP catalogue record for this book is available from the British Library

ISBN   978 1 84842 026 7

FSC
Mixed Sources
Product group from well-managed
forests and other controlled sources
Cert no. SGS-COC-2953
www.fsc.org
© 1996 Forest Stewardship Council

Parlour Song was first performed by the Atlantic Theater Company, New York, on 15 February 2008, with the following cast:

DALE   Jonathan Cake
NED   Chris Bauer
JOY   Emily Mortimer

Director   Neil Pepe
Set Designer   Robert Brill
Costume Designer   Sarah Edwards
Lighting Designer   Kenneth Posner
Sound Designer   Obadiah Eaves
Projection Designer   Dustin O'Neil

The play received its European premiere at the Almeida Theatre, London, on 19 March 2009, with the following cast:

DALE   Andrew Lincoln
NED   Toby Jones
JOY   Amanda Drew

Director   Ian Rickson
Designer   Jeremy Herbert
Lighting Designer   Peter Mumford
Sound Designer   Paul Groothuis
Composer   Stephen Warbeck

Characters

NED, *forty*

DALE, *forty*

JOY, *forty*

Setting

England, in the late summer/autumn. In and around the small suburban new-built home of Ned and Joy.

This text went to press before the end of rehearsals for the European premiere and so may differ slightly from the play as performed.

Darkness. Silence. Spotlight on:

DALE. It started small.

Blackout.

In the air, apocalyptic visions appear: buildings, towers, skyscrapers crashing to the ground; office blocks, factories, entire community projects collapsing; histories imploding, destroyed, erased for ever, disappearing in dust as the music swells to utter darkness and silence.

NED *and* JOY's *house*. NED. DALE. *A TV.* NED *at the controls.*

DALE. Fuck me. (*Beat.*) Look at that. (*Shakes head.*) Where are we?

NED. Leeds. A cooling tower outside Leeds.

DALE. Where were you?

NED. The Buffer Zone.

DALE. The where?

NED. You got three areas. The Designated Drop Area, or DDA. That's the sector where the main body of the structure is primed to fall. Then you got the PDA. The Predicted Debris Area: namely the maximum area in which fragment equals S and/or debris can reasonably be expected. You calculate the height, weight, materials, foundations, weather conditions, crunch them, and you get a number. Then it's standard safety procedure to build an eight to ten per cent comfort zone into the number. That gives you your PDA. So you've got the

DDA, the PDA, then you got a Buffer Zone. I'm in the Buffer Zone. It's the safe area. You're completely safe there. Nothing's going to hurt you in the Buffer Zone.

A surtitle appears:

'Everything is disappearing.'

NED. Anyway, that's all boring, technical stuff.

DALE. Boring?

NED. It's technical –

DALE. Do you want to swap?

NED. What? No I just –

DALE. Do you want to swap jobs, Ned?

NED. No it's just –

Okay. Please. My CV…? Just to… hang on… Since school. Kitchen porter. Skivvy. Dogsbody –

NED. Dale –

DALE. Withering period of unemployment… Australia. Back home. Disaster with Tanya. Back to my mum's. Little Chef manager… Washing cars. Nowhere in all that did they give me a thousand tons of TNT and a fucking great big plunger and say, 'See that factory over there… Really, and I mean really, fuck it up.' 'See that tower block? We don't want one brick left standing on another… Don't come back till you've fully damaged it.' Do they have a big plunger? They do, don't they. Big comedy. (*Mimes a plunger.*) They do. I knew it. I wash cars. Cars, Ned.

NED. Dale –

DALE. Kids' cars. Wankers' cars.

NED. How many car washes you got. Three? Four? How many do you employ? Twenty, thirty blokes.

DALE. Kosovans, Ned. Twenty or thirty Poles. You ask for a Kit Kat, they come back with the *Daily Mail*.

NED. You've built that business. That's a good solid local –

DALE. Cars, Ned. Wankers' cars. You have a fight with the missus. Money worries. Whoosh. Lo the heavens shake with thunder. What have I got, I'm feeling the pressure. A sponge, Ned. A squeegee. A bucket of dirty water.

NED. At the end of the day –

DALE. At the end of the day, Ned, I've got pruny fingers. You've got a thousand-foot dust cloud, and a clatter you can hear ten miles away. The end of the fuckin' world.

NED. I forgot to say. I'm going to be in the paper.

DALE. When?

NED. *Advertiser*.

DALE. See?

NED. Not just me. The whole team.

DALE. See? My point exactly. What for. Is it a… (*Mimes plunger.*)

NED. Big job. Local.

DALE. You lucky sod. Tell me.

NED. It's hush-hush.

DALE. Tell me.

NED. I can't.

DALE. Tell me anyway.

NED. It's the Arndale Centre.

　　Pause.

DALE. You're blowing up the Arndale Centre?

NED. Yes.

DALE. Fuck me. The Arndale Centre.

NED. Six weeks Tuesday.

DALE. Why?

NED. It's obsolete.

DALE. I do all my shopping there. Everybody does.

NED. Its days are numbered, Dale. There's going to be a photo-graph. Of us. The team. In front of the Arndale. Then another. Of it gone. At least that's how I'd do it.

DALE. Front page?

NED. Could be. Should be.

DALE. Should be on the telly.

NED. My lips are sealed.

DALE. You bastard.

NED. No comment.

DALE. You rotter. Are you going to be on the box?

NED. It's just a bit of fun really. It's eye-candy, isn't it. Tomorrow's fish-and-chip paper.

DALE. Well, that's that. It's going to cost a pound to talk to you. (*Beat.*) Do you know what? I could do this all day.

NED. Where you going? We haven't finished. I was just going to get another –

DALE. Mate –

NED. I was just going to get another one.

DALE. It's not me. You know it's not me. It's Lyn –

NED. You got time for one more. Quick one.

DALE. Lyn'll be on the warpath.

NED. Five minutes.

DALE. Oooh… He always does this…

NED. Okay? Are you… just… are you ready?

DALE. Oooh… He always does this…!

NED. Okay? Falkirk Industrial Estate, 2002. We drop this gas-works and there's literally zero backwash.

DALE. Ned –

NED. I've got it upstairs. I know exactly where it is. I've got them all alphabetised.

DALE. Ned –

NED. I could have found it by now.

DALE. Ned –

NED. Come on. What's five minutes? We could have watched it by now.

DALE. Ned. I've seen it. (*Beat.*) Ned, mate, I've seen it. You showed me it. Last week.

Pause.

NED. When?

DALE. Last week. You showed me all of these last week.

NED. No I never.

DALE. Yes you did.

NED. When?

DALE. Last week.

NED. That was Pete. From the pub.

DALE. No it wasn't.

NED. It was Pete from the pub.

DALE. Ned. Yes. Ned. You showed them to Pete from the pub. You also showed them to me. Last week. And the week before that. With Rodge. And Nobby. Who'd seen it the week before that. With me. Who'd seen it three times the week before that. Once with Nobby. Once with Rodge. Once with Pete from the pub. What I'm saying is, what I'm getting at is, we've seen it. I've seen it.

NED. I'm sure you haven't seen Falkirk.

DALE. Ned –

NED. In fact I'm positive you haven't seen Falkirk. You're thinking of Kilmarnock. The block of flats in –

DALE. Not the block of flats in Kilmarnock. Although I know it well.

NED. There's no way you've seen –

DALE. Ned –

DALE. There's no way you've seen Fal –

DALE. It's raining. There's a bagpipe band. A countdown by the local lady mayor. A Mrs Bridey McNeil. Just when she starts, a kid jumps out the crowd and gets his bum out –

NED. That shouldn't have happened –

DALE. There's the countdown. Then you blow it up. (*Pause.*) It's jaw-dropping. No one's saying it's not.

Silence.

NED. Of course. Of course. I remember. I remember now.

Pause.

DALE. Ned. Tell me to fuck off…

NED. I'm fine.

DALE. Good. Good. Excellent. Tell me to –

NED. Dale –

DALE. Good. Splendid. I was just, you know… Mates 'n' all.

NED. Hey –

DALE. You'd tell me if something was –

NED. Hey. Dale. We're mates.

DALE. Mates. Exactly. No harm done.

NED. None taken.

DALE. Well, I best be off.

NED. Yeah, I better be getting on as well.

DALE. Thanks for the… what's the word?

NED. Biscuits.

DALE. Carnage.

NED. It's a bit of fun.

DALE. Exactly.

NED. Catch you later, Dale.

DALE. Thanks for the biscuits –

NED. Everything's disappearing.

    Pause.

DALE. What?

    Pause.

NED. What? Nothing.

DALE. You said. (*Beat.*) You just said –

NED. You best be off.

DALE. 'Everything's disappearing.'

NED. Mind how you go.

    Pause.

DALE. All right, mate. See you around.

NED. Not if I see you first.

    Pause. DALE *turns to go. He turns back.*

DALE. Ned. (*Beat. Looks at watch.*) Look. (*Beat.*) Life isn't always… (*Beat.*) I mean… I'm not a doctor. Not a doctor. What's the word? Gandalf. Not Gandalf. Like Gandalf. My point is, life is like a river. Things change. For us as for the river. See, one day they may build a bridge over the river. And you know. A cycle path. There may be an industrial leak that wipes out all the fish. They didn't see it coming. How could they? They're but fish, Ned. My point is, things changeth. 'Twas ever thus. Soothsayer. Bollocks. That's the one. What?

NED. No. I mean… Everything's disappearing. From my house.

DALE. What?

NED. My stuff. My possessions… they're disappearing.

DALE. What are you talking about?

NED. I mean my belongings. My things. The things I own. My stuff. Dale, if I tell you something, do you swear you will never tell another soul?

DALE. I promise.

NED. Swear to me. Swear on your life.

DALE. Ned. What's wrong. What's the story?

Blackout.

Spotlight on:

DALE. So like I said. It started small. A pocketwatch. Old set of golf clubs. Box camera. Pair of silver-backed hairbrushes. See, Ned's a demolition expert. He goes away. On business, all the time. Up North. Wales. South East. Wherever they need something blowing up. How it worked, he'd go away for a few days, when he came back something else was missing. A set of spanners. Screwdrivers. Stuff he picked up at a car-boot sale. Tins. Old train set he had when he was a kid. Old cricket bat. Model cars. Drill bits. Drill. Knives. Now... I know Ned. My first thought was he's got his knickers in a bunch. See, Ned's a squirrel. He squirrels stuff away. Go in the man's garage. Aladdin's cave? Man goes to a house auction, buys three old sinks. Three old bog cisterns. Five old toasters. You walk in his garage, shed, his attic, you wouldn't find a Sherman tank, but he swears he's got a system. Knows where everything is. (*Beat*.) I asked him if anyone else had a set of keys. He said there was only ever two sets. His set, which he always, always kept on him. And her set. His missus. His wife. Joy.

Blackout.

A surtitle appears:

'Face it. It's a dead duck.'

NED *and* JOY*'s house. Both at a table, eating.*

NED. Well, that's that. Sixty days straight without rain. That has never happened before in the entire history of here. Last day of July it was. I was in the greenhouse. Killing greenfly. Suddenly the sky turns black. 'Hello,' says I. 'So long summer. Here comes Old Jack Frost.' How wrong can you be? It better break soon because I'll tell you this much. It's not natural. It's unnatural. Mother Nature is Not a Happy Bunny. (*Beat*.) How's the bird? Is it moist enough? I rested it. That's the secret. Remove the bird. On one side, tin foil. Ten, fifteen minutes. Give it a rest. It has to relax. You can't forget you're eating muscle. Is it okay, Joy?

JOY. It's lovely.

NED. There's a leg left. Little leg? Or a wing. Little wing? You sure? It's not dry? How are the carrots? Overdone?

JOY. They're lovely.

NED. You sure you don't want more?

JOY. This is perfect.

NED. There's a leg left. Little leg. You sure. A wing? Little wing? There's more peas…

JOY. It's lovely, Ned. The bird, it's moist. The roast potatoes are crispy outside, fluffy inside. The carrots are sweet and crunchy. The gravy is lip-smacking, and the peas are perfection. And the best bit is, it's exactly the right size portion.

Pause. NED *starts to laugh.*

NED. This'll make you laugh. I'm driving over Langley Marsh, where we blew up that cement works last spring. You'll never guess what they've gone and done. They've built seventy-eight houses on that site. And every single house is the same as ours. Same layout. Same front door. So I think why not? I'll stop off. Have a nose around. Being nosey. Pop my nose in, in the kitchen and guess what? It's our kitchen. Same units. Same taps. Cloakroom. Same sink. Same fittings. Lounge-diner, exactly the same. Same floor. Same hatch. Except for… (*Laughs.*) Except for this bloody great rat. In the middle of the room. Huge it was. Like a dog. Long. Sleek. Tail like a rope. Staring at me. Not moving. Mind you, that's building sites. You drop a biscuit, half a pork pie, that'll bring fifty. Normally they see you and scarper. Not this chap. Blimey, he was big. Massive, massive rodent. Makes you think, don't it.

Pause.

JOY. What about?

NED. What? Sorry?

JOY. What does it make you think about?

NED. What do you mean?

JOY. You seen this big rat. Said it makes you think. (*Pause.*)
What about?

Pause.

NED. Well, you know. About...

Pause.

JOY. Rats?

NED. No. What? No. Not just... No. (*Laughs.*) It's not about
rats. No. (*Beat.*) Well, yes. Yes. It is. It's about rats.

JOY. It is, isn't it...?

NED. I didn't explain myself. You had to be there.

JOY. I miss out on everything, me.

Silence.

NED. By the way. We got the Arndale job.

JOY. The what?

NED. The Arndale job.

JOY. What Arndale job?

NED. The Arndale Centre in town. We're knocking it down.

JOY. Why?

NED. It's being redeveloped.

JOY. Says who?

NED. The council. We got the contract.

JOY. You're knocking down the Arndale Centre.

NED. We're going to be in the paper.

JOY. But I do all my shopping there. I'm always in the Arndale
Centre. The chemist is there. The newsagent's is there.
Tesco's is there. That's where I go. That's where I shop.

NED. Fear not. It's being replaced.

JOY. What with?

NED. The New Arndale Centre.

JOY. What's wrong with the old one?

NED. It's obsolete.

JOY. Says who?

NED. The People. The People want bigger and better.

JOY. Which People?

NED. The People of this town, Joy. The People want flexible shopping solutions. Twenty-four-hour. A spa. Softplay. And more car parking. Ours is not to reason why, Joy. It's a relic. An eyesore. It's no longer viable.

JOY. What does that mean?

NED. It means we're knocking it down.

JOY. No you're bloody not.

NED. Joy. We're a demolition company. We don't just drive round choosing buildings to blow up. The council confers. Did you know there was a forest right here? Five years ago. Right where you're sitting. It was here for a thousand years. Now it's gone. We're here. Everything has its time, Joy. And time is up for the Arndale Centre. Face it. It's a dead duck.

JOY. Well. This calls for a celebration.

She fills his glass. Raises hers.

Congratulations, Edward.

NED. By the way, have you seen my cufflinks?

Beat.

JOY. What?

NED. My cufflinks. The gold ones. The ones you gave me.

JOY. They're in your drawer.

NED. Right. Right.

JOY. They're always in your drawer, Edward. That's where they live.

NED. Right. But you see. I had a good root around. And I couldn't find them.

JOY. Well, when did you last have them?

NED. That wedding.

JOY. What wedding?

NED. Your cousin Anne's. In Gants Hill.

JOY. That was June last year.

NED. Must be.

JOY. That was over a year ago.

NED. That was the last time I wore them. That was the last occasion I wore cufflinks.

JOY. Well, this is splendid.

NED. What?

JOY. Those are twenty-four-carat solid-gold cufflinks, Edward.

NED. I know.

JOY. Oh you know, do you? Who was it got the train into Hatton Garden and spent all day picking them out? Who got them engraved by the engraver to the Queen? Do you remember what it said on them?

NED. Joy –

JOY. I worked double shifts all spring to pay for them. This is splendid. Thank you very much, Edward. You've made my day.

NED. I'm sure they'll turn up.

JOY. I'm glad you're so confident.

NED. They'll be somewhere silly.

JOY. You've made my day.

NED. You know me. I'd lose my head if it wasn't screwed on.

Pause.

JOY. Well, that was delicious, Edward.

NED. Hang about, I've made a sweet.

JOY. I've not got the room.

NED. I've made jam roly-poly.

JOY. I couldn't possibly. I'm full up.

NED. You sure? Couldn't squeeze some in?

JOY. I'd love to but it's physically impossible. I'm stuffed. It's your fault. You've filled me up.

NED. But there's always a sweet. I always make a sweet.

JOY. I'm already in discomfort, Ned. You don't want me in more discomfort, do you.

NED. Of course not, Joy.

JOY *stands up.*

JOY. Compliments to the chef, Edward. I'm going to bed.

NED. It's nine o'clock.

JOY. I don't feel well.

NED. Cripes. Was it the food?

JOY. The food was fine.

NED. Was it the gravy? Was the gravy too rich?

JOY. The gravy was perfect. I need to lie down.

NED. Well, goodnight, my cuddly toy. Perhaps when I come up, we could play Scrabble. Would you like that? Little game of Scrabble?

Beat.

JOY. Goodnight, Edward.

NED. Sleep tight. (*Beat*.) My little cuddly toy.

She heads out.

Joy.

JOY. What?

NED. I remember. What it said on the cufflinks. I remember.

He watches her leave.

Blackout.

Spotlight on:

DALE. Me and Lyn, Ned and Joy, we live six feet apart. It's the
same house. But round theirs, everything's backwards.
You're in our lounge, you need a slash, come out, do a left.
Do that next door, you end up in the kitchen. It's a nice area.
Young couples. Families. You've not got to drive far to see a
cow. But like any nice area now, you've not got to drive far
before you're in the fucking Dark Ages. You can see them
from the end of the garden. Six black blocks, on the horizon.
Hatfield Towers. I know they haven't got it easy over there.
And there's some good people. Some good, hard-working
folk. And some right maggots. Their kids don't give a fuck.
They come in the car wash, some spotty little orc in a brand-
new Boxster. And the nine-year-olds. We had stinkbombs
and snappits. This lot've got crossbows. Muskets. Poison
darts. So I said to Ned, check your locks and windows, mate.
Could be a sneak thief. Someone from over there. From
Middle Earth, some twelve-year-old can inch in through a
bog window. Some four-stone kid they can grease up and
feed in through the letterbox. But Ned said, why would
someone steal a stamp collection and leave the Xbox. Walk

past three tellies to nick a box of Victorian postcards out the attic, the Collected Works of H.G. Wells, an Edwardian clay-pipe collection, a stuffed badger and a bronze bust of Aldous Huxley. And I had to admit it didn't add up. (*Beat*.) But you have to know Ned. What is Ned? I don't want to say paranoid. But on a good day, on the flat, he's volatile. Fragile. Sometimes, when he gets an idea, it doesn't always wash through. It plants itself. It stays there and it grows and grows and ripens. And then it starts to go off. It starts to fester. (*Beat*.) Two months back, the doorbell goes. Seven in the morning. It's Ned. Dressed for work. He looks terrible. Hasn't slept. Three, four nights on the bounce. Big bags. Shivers. He comes in the kitchen, I'm making tea, and I turn round to hand him a cuppa and he's fast asleep. On his feet. I touch him and he wakes up, takes the tea and drinks it down, boiling hot. Straight out of the kettle. Doesn't even notice. Doesn't flinch. Then he looks at me square in the eye and says, 'Dale, I am fat. I want to get fit. Tone up.' I like to keep fit. I know the ropes. So I say, 'Why not? Let's devise a program. Get you match fit. Tight. Tough. Back in shape. Can't hurt, can it?'

Blackout.

A surtitle appears:

'Each year, the birds came back.'

NED *and* JOY*'s house*. NED *and* DALE, *warming up. Stretches. They stop. Facing each other.*

DALE. How you feeling?

NED. Good. Loose.

DALE. You ready?

NED. Ready to rock, Dale.

DALE. Ready to work.

NED. Bring it on, Dale. Rock and roll.

DALE. Okay. On your back.

> DALE *lies on his back*. NED *does too*.

> Feet six inches off the floor. Thirty seconds. Go. (*Beat*.) How's that feel?

NED. Instantly awful. Instantly wrong.

DALE. Push on.

NED. Terribly terribly wrong. Like I'm going to puke. And possibly soil myself.

DALE. Breathe. In. Out. In. Out. Twenty more seconds.

NED. My God. Make it stop. Make it stop, Dale. Please make it stop.

DALE. And rest.

> NED *collapses*.

> Are you okay?

> NED *is panting*. *He starts crying*.

NED. I'm sorry, Dale. FUCK!

DALE. Ned –

NED. Fuck it.

DALE. Ned –

NED. I tensed up. I've been building up to this all day.

DALE. Calm down.

NED. I've had a shocker there.

DALE. Okay, Ned. Stand up. Ned. Relax. Stand up. We'll take it slowly.

NED. I'm sorry, Dale.

DALE. We'll start again. We'll try something else. Just do this.
On the spot. (*He starts a ropeless skipping motion.*) One
foot then the next. Just copy me. Until I ask you to rest.
Okay?

NED. Got it.

DALE. Keep breathing. In. Out.

He starts skipping.

How is that?

NED. Fine.

DALE. Good.

NED. Just like this?

DALE. Just like that.

NED. Cor. Feels great to blow the cobwebs out.

DALE. Tell me your goals.

NED. Basically I'm looking for core fitness. Strength. Stamina.
And I want to lose the tits. I'm not worried about the legs.
Fuck the legs. Ignore them. I just want to look, you know.
Normal. Alive. Without tits.

DALE. So just talk normally. Okay? What were you saying
before? When we came in.

NED. Where were we?

DALE. Gloucester. A five-star hotel in Gloucester.

NED. Right. Gloucester. Five-star country mansion. Michelin
restaurant. Spa. Four-poster. We've just had a massage, or
I've had massage, and Joy's had a facial, whatever, we're
feeling well blissed out and we've got a couple of hours to
kill before we go up in this balloon. (*Off* DALE*'s look.*) It's
the honeymoon package. You get a four-poster bed, your
food, a set number of spa treatments, and a go in a balloon.
Sunset balloon trip. England at sunset. Bird's eye view.
Champagne and that.

DALE. And rest. That sounds regal. That is a regal package. Keep talking. Go again in thirty seconds.

NED. So we've got a couple of hours to kill before the balloon trip. I suggest a stroll. I suggest a walk round Gloucester. I've heard it's nice.

DALE. I've heard it's nice.

NED. The centre's nice. Olde worlde.

DALE. That's the Romans for you.

NED. So we park and ride, and we're walking round Gloucester, and it is nice, find the cathedral, that's nice, pop our heads in, light a candle, feeling blissed-out after the massage. Facial.

DALE. Whatever…

NED. Anyway, we're walking down the high street, and suddenly I see this thing blowing towards us down the pavement. And I bend down and pick it up and it's a fifty-pound note.

DALE. Bollocks.

NED. On my life. A nifty.

DALE. Get in!

NED. Just blowing down the street. Just blowing along the pavement.

DALE. Get in! (*Looking at watch.*) Go.

They start skipping again.

NED. So I have a shufty round and no one's looking distraught, no one's patting themselves down, having kittens, shouting for the fuzz… so I think, 'Result,' and I stick it in my pocket. So I say to Joy, you know, 'What shall we do with it?' And Joy turns to me, it's this lovely sunny day, and she turns to me, and she says this brilliant, really touching thing…

DALE. Oh no. Don't…

NED. What?

DALE *stops*.

DALE. She didn't. Tell me she didn't make you hand it in.

NED. Wait. Wait. No. She doesn't. She doesn't say that. She
says... She says this fantastically romantic thing.

NED *stops*.

She says that it's a sign. From the gods. From God. Or
whatever, blessing our nuptials. And she said to honour the
gods, whatever, we should take half each and go and buy each
other a present. Something spontaneous, you know, that we'd
remember for ever, to remember this moment by. Like if you
saw it in ten years' time or whatever, it would nourish us.

You know, when you think of... Just two people... in
Gloucester... walking down the street...

DALE. Amazing. Magical.

NED. Just two normal people, find this money...

DALE. Get in!

NED. It's amazing. And then she says that...

DALE. It's a moment. It becomes a moment...

NED. Spontaneous –

DALE. With the money.

NED. Exactly. But it's not about the money.

DALE. Ned. Come on. Of course it's not. It's the magical...

NED. Exactly.

DALE. The magical mystery...

NED. Exactly. So we buy a Yorkie, something, Juicy Fruit,
break it for change, and agree to meet back in an hour
outside Argos.

DALE. I like this. I like this story.

They start skipping again.

NED. So here I am, walking around Gloucester with this big
smile on my face, thinking, this is great. I am a man. On his
honeymoon. I'm on my own but it's a lovely day, and I'm
somewhere in this old town, and there's a woman walking
around performing this magical task, on a quest to honour
me. And I shall honour her.

DALE. Plus you've got the balloon ride to look forward to.

NED. Yeah, but I'm not thinking about the balloon ride at this
point.

DALE. Of course not. You're lost in the moment. You're in the
zone. I like this story. I like it a lot.

NED. So I start browsing. Pop in a couple of antique shops,
because my first thought was get her something old. I just
thought. Gloucester. Olde Worlde. Something classic. Something with soul.

DALE. With…

NED. With a past…

DALE. Character…

NED. A treasure… Exactly. I'm looking at all these bits and
bobs. Trinkets, whatnot, but nothing's leaping out.

DALE. Whoops.

NED. I go from shop to shop. Nothing's leaping out.

DALE. I didn't like to say but you're going to struggle. In most
antique shops with twenty-five sheets –

NED. I can't find anything…

DALE. What are we talking, realistically? Some old bottle?
Some tin? 'It's filled with the patina of a bygone era.' Really.
It's a piece of leather, you nit. It's a leather strap. And, you
don't even know what it's off. Can I stop you, Ned? Two
words. Victoria's Secrets.

NED. What?

DALE. If that was me with twenty-five sheets I'd get straight up Victoria's Secrets. Up the minty end. Get something really cheap and minty.

NED. Dale –

DALE. It's my honeymoon, Ned. There's no better time. 'There you go, love. I'll give you something to... fuckin'... nourish...' (*Beat.*) Ignore me. Please. Carry on. Please. I like this story. Ignore me.

Beat. NED sighs. Soldiers on.

NED. Now I don't know Gloucester. So I go round this one corner, and suddenly, the shops have stopped. I've run out of shops.

DALE. And rest.

DALE stops. NED too.

NED. I'm walking out of Gloucester. And I don't know why, but I didn't turn round. I just kept on walking. It's just petrol stations and roundabouts. Then the countryside. It's like I'm in a dream. But I can't stop walking. (*Beat.*) So I'm at this roundabout, fourth or fifth out of town. I come across this yard. And it's just this Portakabin, and this old bloke selling all these objects. Stone things. Things made out of stone. Wood things. Garden seats. Benches. And I'm suddenly drawn to this blue tarpaulin. And this is mad, but I thought, whatever it is I'm getting her, it's under that blue tarpaulin over there, in the rain. So I go over. And I lift the tarpaulin. And underneath, there's this beautiful, soapstone birdbath. Really simple, but beautiful. Not fussy, just beautifully proportioned. Simple. Perfect. So I knock on the Portakabin and I ask the man how much it is for the birdbath. And he says it's twenty-five pounds. (*Beat.*) On my life. That birdbath, the one over there, under the blue tarp, is twenty-five pound.

Pause.

DALE. Did you haggle?

Pause.

NED. What?

DALE. You didn't haggle?

NED. You're missing the point, Dale. It's twenty-five pounds.

Pause.

DALE. Of course. The fuckin'... The magical mystery twenty-five pounds.

NED. Exactly. It's perfect. So I buy it. But now I've got ten minutes to lug it all the way back into Gloucester. It weighs a fucking ton.

DALE. Fuckin'... Rocky. Go on, my son.

NED. I'm telling you, Dale. It weighs A TON.

DALE. Fuck off. It's the magic birdbath. It's light as a feather.

NED. It weighs a fucking ton.

DALE. I don't care. Put your back into it.

NED. I've got to dead lift a stone birdbath half a mile back into town. So I get back there, absolutely shagged –

DALE. Sweating like a dogger...

NED. Pouring... pouring with sweat and I show it her. And she looks at it, and I know straight away it's perfect. She's got tears in her eyes. And when we moved into our house, the first thing we did, we put that birdbath in the garden. And on that first morning when we woke up, there was this pair of chaffinches perched on it, drinking from it. And every single morning when we woke up, we'd go and sit by the window, before breakfast and watch the birds. Robins, finches, warblers, tits, we'd get up really early in the morning, on a spring morning, we'd watch the birds splashing in the water, watch them preening, dancing for each other, in little pairs, each pair perfect. And each year, the birds came back, and each year it was the same. (*Pause.*) Yeah. So anyway, I come out this morning, and it's gone. It's... the birthbath has gone. There's just a white patch of grass. It's disappeared.

Pause.

DALE. Ned –

NED. It's a birdbath, Dale. A twenty-five-quid birdbath. Our fence is eight foot high. The gate's padlocked. It's a soap-stone birdbath. It weighs a fucking ton. I should know. I've lugged it clean across Gloucester.

Pause. DALE's *watch alarm goes off.*

DALE. And rest. (*Pause.*) How long have you been married, Ned?

NED. Eleven years.

DALE. How are things?

NED. Things?

DALE. Things.

Beat.

NED. Things. (*Beat.*) Good.

DALE. Good.

NED. Good.

DALE. Good. I'm just kicking the tyres.

NED. Exactly. Good. (*Nods.*)

Pause.

DALE. Recently...?

Pause.

NED. Recently? Recently. (*Nods.*) Recently less good. Recently... not so good. Recently not good.

DALE. Good.

Silence.

NED. Few years back... We used to spend all day in bed.
Drinking tea. Playing Scrabble. Then... you know...
Between games. All day long. Five, sometimes six games of
Scrabble. Sometimes we'd play Sexy Scrabble. If you could
spell it, you could have it. I once got forty-five points for
'blow-job' on a triple-word score.

DALE *laughs.* NED *laughs. He stops laughing.*

Then we stopped. We haven't played in years. I'm not sure
I'd even remember the rules.

Pause.

DALE. Year or two back. Lyn and me. In the boudoir. Major
tumbleweed.

NED. Whoops.

DALE. Move along. Nothing to see.

NED. Whoops-a-daisy.

DALE. In the end I bought this tape. This doctor lady. New
approaches. Techniques. I used to listen to it on the way to
the car wash. I've still got it somewhere. I could dig it out.

NED. Thanks, Dale. I don't think so.

DALE. If you change your mind. But I warn you. This doctor
lady. She's dirty. She's deeply filthy. Medical website? Not a
bit of it. There's stuff on there would make a sailor blush.

NED. Thanks, Dale.

DALE. Well, if you change your mind.

Pause.

What did she get you?

NED. What?

DALE. With the magic twenty-five pound.

Beat.

NED. A tie. (*Pause.*) A tie with air balloons on.

Blackout.

Spotlight on:

DALE. Maybe it is. Maybe it isn't. Fine. Yes. At the end of the day, even if it's true… A pocketwatch? Lawnmower? A stuffed badger? That's not it. That's not the problem. That's not why he can't sleep. Shakes. When I let the dog out at four in the morning, he's out there, on his back lawn, staring out over the fence. Sometimes he goes a week, two weeks, without so much as a wink. Makes him antsy. Jumpier than a crow on roadkill. Because he doesn't sleep. He has black moods. Forgets things. Gets confused. Imagines things. And so it goes round. I said to him, I said, 'Go down the doctor, get some pills. Sort it out.' But, see, Ned's a blaster. A D-Man. He handles high explosives, week in, week out. If a D-Man's got anything more than a sniffle he can't go to his GP. They knew you was on the sleepers, or the happy pills, they wouldn't let you blow up a bouncy castle. So he's got no choice, just got to white-knuckle it. Bite down. Wait for morning. And I tell you one thing. Joy don't know. She don't know about the sleeping. (*Beat.*) Joy don't know the half of it.

Blackout.

A surtitle appears:

'An unquenchable thirst.'

NED *and* JOY*'s bedroom.* NED *is in bed, with headphones on.*

VOICE. Performing cunnilingus can be one of the most wonderful things you can do for a woman.

Sounds of a women getting excited. NED *listens.*

Leaving your tongue soft and your jaw relaxed, try licking from her vaginal entrance up to her clitoris, and following the outer edges of her vagina along both sides. This works as a great ice-breaker. (*He frowns.*) So. Exercise one. Stick your tongue as far out of your mouth as possible. (*He does.*) Slowly, curl the tip up and down. And side to side. All the time focus on your partner, and the intense pleasure only you are delivering. Before long, she just won't be able to help herself keep coming back for more. And don't forget, a great lover's hands never stop moving.

He starts to move his hands.

Next, the tongue tube. Roll your tongue into a tube and slide it back and forth. This is likely to bring any woman to a volcanic orgasm.

NED, *tongue out, waving his hands like Al Jolson, when* JOY *enters from the bathroom.* NED *deftly morphs his movement into a dance, as if enjoying a particularly funky tune. She watches him, lost in music.*

NED (*presses stop on the tape*). Clapton. You are a god. Timeless. Absolutely timeless.

JOY *walks over to a chair and removes her stockings.* NED *watches.*

Listen to that same dry westerly. It's raining somewhere in America right now, and they said on the radio that that is actually our rain. Well, it better break soon because – (*Beat.*) What's that?

JOY. What's what?

NED. On your finger. What is it?

JOY. It's a plaster.

NED. Oh dear. You have accident? Little accident?

JOY. I cut myself.

NED. How?

JOY. Chopping lemons.

NED. Lemons? Looks nasty. I bet it bled. Did it bleed? My little cuddly –

JOY. Ned. We need to talk.

NED. What about?

JOY. What are these?

She is holding some pills.

NED. What? I don't know.

JOY. What do you mean you don't know?

NED. I've never seen them before.

JOY. Then how did they get in your cabinet?

NED. Hang about. Oh them. They're nothing.

JOY. Where did you get these pills, Edward?

NED. Nowhere.

JOY. Nowhere.

NED. They're nothing. They're just… (*Pause.*) They're… vitamins.

JOY. They don't look like vitamins.

NED. That's because they're special vitamins, Joy.

JOY. Where did you get them?

NED. I don't want to discuss it. They're private. Some things are private and they're… they're private. (*Low, to himself.*) Layla. You got me on my knees. (*To her.*) What are you doing in my cabinet anyway?

JOY. Where did you get them, Edward?

NED. On the internet. Happy now?

JOY. Where on the internet?

NED. A website.

JOY. You're aware that it says in your contract that if you take any mood-altering drugs –

NED. Joy –

JOY. – emotional labicity stabilisers sleeping pills or prescription analgaesics –

NED. Please, Joy –

JOY. – then you have to declare them to your employers. If you don't you are liable to random testing and if you test positive you are suspended without pay. Then we default on our mortgage payments, and if we do that for three to six months then we'll lose the house. We have nothing. No money. No job. No house. Now what are these pills, Edward? And think very carefully before you answer.

NED. They're vitamins.

JOY. They're not vitamins.

NED. They are. They're a blend of vitamins and a tonic.

JOY. What type of tonic?

NED. I don't know. A pick-me-up.

JOY. Ned. What have you been taking?

NED. They're private. Okay? They're to do with me.

JOY. Ned –

NED. Leave me alone.

JOY. Edward.

NED. They're Rogaine.

Silence.

JOY. Rogaine? (*Beat.*) Hair pills.

NED. Happy now?

JOY. You're taking hair pills.

NED. Happy now, Joy?

JOY. Why are you taking hair pills?

NED. I don't know. Happy now?

JOY. Why –

NED. Look, can we… To have hair. Okay?

She laughs.

JOY. Why?

NED. I don't know. To have it. To have some. Okay?

JOY. Oh, Ned. But… You're bald.

NED. I'm aware of that.

JOY. You've never had hair.

NED. Actually. Yes I did.

JOY. Not since I've known you. On our first date you were bald. You're bald in the wedding photos. You've always been bald.

NED. I had hair. I had hair before. I did exist before. And when I did, I had hair.

JOY. But not for years.

NED. But I had it. I had it. Okay? And maybe I want some now.

She laughs.

What?

JOY. Nothing.

NED. What's so funny?

JOY. Nothing.

NED. Then why are you laughing?

JOY. How many do you take?

NED. Stop laughing at me, Joy.

JOY. How long have you been taking them?

NED. That's none of your business. Six months.

JOY. Ooh, love. You want to get your money back, love.

She laughs.

NED. Guess what? I went out to the shed this morning and guess what? The lawnmower's gone.

She stops laughing. Pause.

Someone's pinched it. Someone's pinched the lawnmower.

JOY. Don't be ridiculous. You can't get in the garden. You put a huge bloody great bike chain on the gate. Last Tuesday.

NED. I know. It's still there.

JOY. Well, how did they get in? More's the point, how the hell did they get it out?

NED. That is the question, Joy. It was there yesterday. I oiled it yesterday, after you asked me to oil it. And sharpen the blades. Said you couldn't bear me squeaking about out there every Sunday. So it was there. But now it's gone. And so have my fishing rods, my toolbox. My dad's beekeeping equipment. But they left your massage chair, your box of bone china, and your knitting machine. And they took the tandem.

JOY. The tandem's gone?

NED. Yes, Joy. Our tandem.

JOY. You bought that for our anniversary. That's a four-hundred-pound, completely unused tandem.

NED. I wanted to use it. I suggested we went on a picnic only last Sunday...

JOY. It looked like rain.

NED. It hasn't rained for seven weeks.

JOY. Hang on. There's a bloody great padlock on the shed. You put it on there only last week.

NED. They broke the padlock. They broke it off with a chisel. The chisel was broke on the floor. It had blood on it. By the way, why were you chopping lemons? (*Pause.*) I just wondered why were you chopping lemons today?

JOY. I was making lemonade.

NED. Lemonade?

JOY. Yes. I woke up this morning with an unquenchable thirst. I'd been dreaming all night about lemonade. All night long I was guzzling gallons of the stuff. I was a pig for it. Couldn't get enough. So this morning, I got up, I got the bus into town and went to the stall in the market and bought all their lemons. I bought six-dozen lemons. I brought them home, lined them up, and took a big knife and sliced the first one in half. Then I was slicing and slicing and squeezing and slicing and squeezing and slicing, and I had accident. I thought I'd cut it off.

NED. Does it hurt? I bet it bled. Did it bleed? I bet it it stung. That explains it then. (*Pause.*) So can I have some?

JOY. Some what?

NED. Some lemonade.

JOY. You've just brushed your teeth.

NED. I can brush them again.

JOY. Don't be ridiculous.

NED. But I can. It's the work of a moment.

JOY. Don't be ridiculous, Edward. Anyway, you can't have any.

NED. Why not?

JOY. It's gone.

NED. Don't tell me you drank it, Joy. Six-dozen lemons.
What's that make. Eh? Two, three gallons. Don't tell me you
drank three gallons of lemonade. There must be some left.
You must've saved me some. You can't have drunk it all.

JOY. Who said I drunk it?

NED. You never drunk it.

JOY. I couldn't drink it.

NED. What?

JOY. You couldn't drink it. It was too tart.

NED. Put sugar in it.

JOY. I did. Then it was too sweet. It was undrinkable. I disposed of it...

NED. You disposed of it.

JOY. I threw it away.

NED. Three gallons of lemonade.

JOY. It was too sweet.

NED. You know me, Joy. I've got a sweet tooth.

JOY. Well, it's too late now. It's down the sink.

Pause.

NED. Is it deep? The cut. What knife was it? The bread knife?
The carving knife? That knife's a killer. Deep, is it? Deep
gash. Bet it throbbed. I hate to think of anything hurting you.

Pause.

JOY. Why don't you kiss it better?

Pause.

NED. Can I, Joy? Can I kiss it better?

JOY. Why don't you?

She holds her hand out.

Kiss it.

He does.

NED. That's better. All better. There there. I bet it bled. Did it bleed, Joy? I bet it did.

Pause.

JOY. It bled something cruel.

Blackout.

Spotlight on:

DALE. I met my wife, Lyn, down the car wash. I'd just started out, my first place. Old burnt-out filling station. Bucket and sponge. This bird pulls up in a little clapped-out Mini. The old sponge, the old leather, splashing suds, soaping it up, wiping it off. All the time she's inside. Doing her make-up. Lipstick. Keeps catching my eye. She's short but buxom. Big. In all the right places. I'm waxing the bonnet, doors, wings, and I see she's left the window open. It's boiling hot, and we're chatting. She's shy. I'm cleaning the boot and she's got the mirror angled, looking at me, putting on bright red lipstick. I've got my shirt off, it's boiling hot. At the end, she says she's left her purse at home. She can't pay me. 'Hello,' thinks I. 'Where's this going. Where's this off to?'

Blackout.

A surtitle appears:

'I tried to grow lemons last year.'

NED *and* JOY*'s house.* JOY *sitting.* DALE *standing.*

DALE. There you go.

JOY. So what was it?

DALE. Trip switch. If there's a surge in the power sometimes it trips out. We've got the same problem over the way. Have you got a torch? In case it happens again.

She flicks a lighter. Lights a cigarette.

Well, if it goes again. It's the white switch above the fusebox. Just flick it up and down three times.

JOY. Three times.

DALE. Up down. Up down. Wait a bit. Up down.

JOY. Up down. Up down. Wait a bit.

DALE. Up down.

JOY. I should be able to manage that.

DALE. I never knew you smoked, Joy.

JOY. I don't.

DALE. Right.

JOY. I used to. Not any more. Only sometimes. Now and then.

DALE. By the way, Lyn asked me to pass on a message. She was popping out, for her nightshift, she said, 'Ask Joy if she fancies a pint.'

JOY. Right.

DALE. Wednesday night. She said you two needed a catch-up. It's been ages.

And I thought, as long as this dry spell keeps up we should have a get-together. Little barbecue. Might as well make the most of it. Before winter takes hold. When's Ned back?

JOY. Friday.

DALE. Where is he this time?

JOY. It's on the fridge.

DALE. He gets around. Scotland. Wales. Yorkshire.

JOY. Tring.

DALE. Tring.

JOY. Tring.

DALE. Not far then. Just up the road...

JOY. No. Not far.

DALE. Is he stopping up that way?

JOY. A Travelodge just off the A38.

DALE. Right. Do you fancy it then? Little barbecue. When he gets back. Just the four of us.

JOY. He's blowing up a kiddies' hospital.

DALE. That should draw a crowd.

JOY. Shall we bring something?

DALE. What?

JOY. To the barbecue.

DALE. Just your good selves. And your world-famous Waldorf salad. Let's just hope the weather holds. If you have any more problems with the...

JOY. Up down. Up down.

DALE. Wait a moment. Up down. If there's any problem. I'm next door. I'll be up for a bit. I'm doing the wages. For the... the Kosovans.

JOY. Well, I shan't keep you.

DALE. Shall I tell Lyn you're on? For Wednesday. A girls' night out.

JOY. Have you got a lemon?

DALE. What? Sorry... A...

JOY. I was just going to make a gin and tonic. I've got gin. And tonic. Ice. I've not got no lemon.

DALE. Let me see. You might be in luck. Lyn went to Lidl's just this afternoon.

JOY. I don't mind replacing it.

DALE. Don't be daft.

JOY. Only if you can spare it.

DALE. Don't be daft.

JOY. Is that all right? It's just I have a craving. For a nice cool gin and tonic. I'll tell you what. If you can spare a lemon, if you give me a lemon, you'll be a lifesaver.

DALE. A lemon.

JOY. A lemon.

Silence.

DALE. Joy.

JOY. I'm thirsty, Dale. Why don't you fetch me a lemon?

Blackout on JOY. *Hold spotlight on:*

DALE. I tried to grow lemons last year. Up the allotment. I was growing the lot. Potatoes. Turnips. Runner beans. It kept getting hotter and hotter. I bought this little lemon tree from the garden centre. Went up every day to water it. Ended up with one rock-hard green bullet. Like a brussel sprout. Then the tree died. It's a desert now, with the drought. I broke my back. Now everything's gone. Just a bare patch of land with a rickety old shed.

Pause.

Spotlight up on JOY.

JOY. I never knew you had an allotment. You're full of surprises.

Well, I'd like to see it.

DALE. See what?

JOY. The allotment.

DALE. Don't be daft. There's nothing there.

JOY. Why don't you show me it?

DALE. When?

JOY. Now.

DALE. But. There's nothing there.

Blackout.

NED *appears in a spotlight. Unblinking.*

NED *and* JOY*'s living room.* NED *is alone. He skips on the spot. Does sit-ups. Ten. Pumping two dumbbells. Press-ups. Star-jumps. Picks up a barbell. Pumps out three. Four. Starts grunting. Shouting. Screaming. Six, seven, eight, nine. Puts it down.*

He puts it down and paces like a wild animal. Throwing punches. Pumped. And starts doing star-jumps. He picks up the fire poker and brandishes it like a sword. Kendo-style. He starts thrashing the sofa. Over and over, in a frenzy. He is about to smash it to pieces when he stops.

He puts the poker down. Suddenly exhausted he collapses onto his back. Breathing hard.

DALE *enters.*

DALE. Ned.

NED. Dale.

DALE. You all right?

NED. I'm good. Resting. Resting between stations.

DALE. Sorry I'm late. I had to fire a couple of Kosovans. You look warm.

NED. I'm hitting the ground running, Dale.

DALE. You've gone very red.

NED. I'm pumped. I'm in the zone.

DALE. Have you drunk any water? Sit down.

NED *removes his shirt.*

NED. Right. Don't hold back. Give it me straight.

Pause.

DALE. Ned –

NED. End-of-week report. Straight Ned. I need feedback. Tell me what you see.

Pause.

DALE. Ned –

NED. From the hip, Dale. Feedback. Hit me.

Long pause.

DALE. Ned. Listen. We're doing great.

NED. Really?

DALE. Yes. Slowly, slowly, catchy monkey.

NED. Hey – Rome wasn't –

DALE. Exactly. A journey of a thousand miles –

NED. How do the tits look?

Beat.

DALE. Great. The tits look great.

NED. Mate. Listen, I'm no fool. I know the score. But, see, last
night I weighed myself. Then I checked on the charts. Last
week, I was morbidly obese. This week, if my sums are
correct, I'm just extremely fat. (*Beat.*) Thank you so much
for this, Dale. You're a real mate. That's great feedback.
Okay. I'm ready.

DALE. What for?

NED. For the test. My body-mass whatsits.

DALE. Index.

NED. Exactly. With the callipers. The pen. Crunch the numbers.

DALE. It's only been one week, Ned.

NED. Exactly. End-of-week report.

DALE. But it'll be much the same.

NED. But it won't be exactly the same. It's got to have moved a
bit. Right?

DALE. Yeah but –

NED. Well, let's test it.

DALE. Ned. It just won't have moved much.

NED. But it will have moved a bit. Christ, I've been killing
myself here. Please test it. I need feedback.

DALE. It's pointless, Ned.

NED. What about the chart?

DALE. The what?

NED. The chart. *Men's Monthly* says keep a chart. So fine. I
have a chart at home. I drew it up on a big piece of graph
paper. Like they said. I bought felt-tip pens. I'm going to
chart my progress and it goes, my chart, it goes week by
week. This is the end of week one. It's time to get on the
chart. Now test my fat.

DALE. Slowly, slowly –

NED. Test my fat.

DALE. Catchy –

NED. Fuck off. Test my fat!

DALE. It takes time, Ned.

NED. I haven't got time, Dale. Now test my fat. Test my fat, Dale. TEST MY FUCKING FAT!

Silence.

I'm sorry.

DALE. It's all right.

NED. What is wrong with me?

DALE. Forget it. Never happened.

NED. What the fuck is wrong with me?

DALE. Shall we move on?

Silence. NED *goes and fetches a book.*

What's that?

NED. This. It's a diary. Have you ever kept a diary, Dale? (*Beat.*) A diary. A journal. You ever a diarist? I do. Not a diary as such. I keep a record of sorts. Every time I go away, stay in a motel, Novotel, bed and breakfast, I have to keep the receipts and they reimburse me each quarter. You've got to be thorough or you never see it back. So I keep a record. Listen to this. Here. (*Reads.*) '12th March. Newbury sevices. A bacon sandwich. Apple turnover. Two bags of cheese and onion. Can of Lilt. Map of Berkshire. *Daily Mail*. Fifteen gallons of four star. £71.10.' (*Beat.*) Funny though. Just reading that, I remember the day perfectly. It chucked it down all day. The M4 was a nightmare. (*Reads.*) '17th March. Room at the Travelodge, Sedgemoor Services, £46. Club sandwich, £3.95. *Gladiator* on pay-per-view, £8.50. Petrol, £29. (*Beat.*) 22nd March. Lunch at The Fight Cocks in St Albans with three local councillors. The rotisserie deluxe for

four people, and wine, £98.60 with a ten-pound tip.' I
remember all these days. Can't remember their names or
nothing. I can see their faces. I can picture them, eating. In
that pub. (*Pause*.) Then it stops. After that, it changes. (*Pause.
Reads*.) 'Monday, 19th April. Made Joy a cuppa. Took it
through from the kitchen to the lounge. Put it on the table in
front of her. She looked up and smiled. "Thanks," she said,
and touched my arm. (*Pause*.) 9th June. Went out into garden.
The sun was setting. Came up behind her. She was staring
out, over the end fence. Put my hand on the small of her back.
She didn't pull away. After ten seconds, she turned, smiled,
and walked inside. (*Pause*.) 21st August. Watching telly. I
laughed at something and Joy laughed too. We both laughed,
together. She put her hand on my thigh as she laughed and
laughed and laughed. (*Pause*.) 1st September. Woke up in
middle of night to find Joy on me. Breathing hard. Sweating
in the moonlight. Hot. Panting. She held me to her. "I want
you," she said. "I want all of you." She ground herself into
me and rode me like never before. A rhythm. A syncopation.
It was like she was in a trance or… yes. Or still asleep. She
never woke up. But she showed a passion like never before.
As she climaxed, she gasped something. I strained close to
her as she croaked out a single word. She said it once. A
name. A place. I don't know. But I know one thing. It wasn't
my name. It wasn't this place.'

DALE. How do you know if you didn't hear it?

NED. I didn't hear it. I felt it. Here. On my cheek. And all I
knew, for sure, was that it didn't belong to me.

DALE. Ned. (*Pause*.) When did you last sleep? How long is it
since you slept?

He walks over. NED *slaps himself on the forehead. There is
something stuck to his forehead.*

What's that?

NED. It's a Scrabble piece. It's the blank, Dale. If you don't
have the right letter, you can use the blank. It can be

anything you want it to be. When I got up this morning, I looked in the mirror and that was on my face. It was stuck to my forehead when I got up this morning. Hello? What's this? Oh look. The blank.

They look at each other.

Who plays Scrabble on their own, Dale? Who plays Scrabble on their own?

Silence.

I love her, Dale. I love her so much. And... I don't know what I'll do. If it's true. (*Beat.*) If it's true. She's not safe.

Blackout.

Projection – extreme close-up on a Scrabble board. We read words:

SPIDER

SUNSHINE

FLYING

SHOES

FURTHER

HONEY

PLEASE

LEMONS

BOOM

GO_DNIGHT

NED *and* JOY*'s bed.* JOY *and* DALE *playing Scrabble. Pause. They both stare down at the board intensely.* JOY *puts a word down. Adds it up.*

JOY. Thirty-one.

DALE. Challenge.

JOY. Dale –

DALE. That's not a word. Challenge.

JOY. Dale.

DALE. That. Trust me. That has got an 'E' in it. That needs an 'E'. Possibly two. Challenge. (*Pause.*) How many letters are left?

JOY. None.

DALE. Bollocks. (*Beat.*) How many do I need?

JOY. A hundred and seventy-three. Give up, Dale.

DALE. Fuck off. I can do this.

JOY. Dale –

DALE. Fuck off. I feel a late surge.

JOY. With Four 'I's and a 'Y'.

DALE. Wait. Stop. How do you know my letters? How do you know what letters I've got?

JOY. I always know what letters you've got.

DALE. How do you know what letters I've got?

JOY. Because when you take them out of the bag, Dale, your lips move. You mouth the letters.

DALE. Bollocks.

JOY. You do. You pull out an 'O' you go 'Ohhh'. 'W'? (*She mouths it.*) Then if you get the blank you usually go 'Yes!'

(*She punches the air.*) The trained eye can pick up on these things. The true Scrabble expert.

DALE. That's cheating.

JOY. Fifteen seconds.

DALE. You don't know my letters.

JOY. Four 'I's and a 'Y'.

DALE. I demand a rematch.

JOY. Ten. Nine. Eight.

DALE. Wait.

JOY. Six. Five. four.

DALE. Okay. Wait. I've got it.

JOY. Three. Two. One.

DALE. Oh no. Earthquake. Earthquake.

DALE *shakes the board till all the letters jump up and down. He then 'pings' the board, pinging all the letters in the air.*

Pause.

What happens now? Remind me.

JOY. Now you go home.

DALE. Why? What did I do?

JOY. It's six.

DALE. I told you. She's got squash.

JOY. Dale –

DALE. She took her squash stuff. She's got squash. She's playing Pauline. With Pauline, it always goes to the wire. It's always a nail-biter. Lyn v Pauline. Call me biased, but Lyn's got Pauline hands-down for flair. But Pauline has it here. (*Taps his head.*) She wins points she shouldn't. Crazy points. Lyn calls her the Terminator. She just keeps coming at you. With that fucking forehand. Lyn v Pauline. It's a war.

JOY. She's dyed her hair.

DALE. Who?

JOY. Last week your wife had black hair. This week she's strawberry blonde.

DALE. Yeah. She looks nice.

JOY. Do you think so? Younger?

DALE. I'd say it brings out her eyes.

JOY. Wouldn't you say it brings out her eyes?

DALE. I would. I'd say it brings out her eyes. Is that a new lamp?

JOY. She came round to show me yesterday morning. She looks sweet. Don't you think she looks sweet? She's bought a new autumn wardrobe. Blacks. Contrasting shades. And two new pairs of shoes. She said she showed the hairdresser a picture of Charlize Theron. Do you think she looks like Charlize Theron, Dale? With her new hairdo. Her new strawberry-blonde hairdo and her autumn wardrobe.

DALE *gets out of bed. Stretches.*

What are you doing?

DALE. Stretching.

He points above the window.

We've got that.

JOY. What?

DALE. That crack above the window. We've got the same crack, but it goes the other way. But we've got that. We've got that crack.

He looks out front, out of the window.

DALE. Fuck me.

JOY. What?

DALE. You can see the motorway from here. Look at that. See, we don't have that. Those fir trees over there are the problem. But look at that. No fir trees. And there it is. Bang. The motorway. (*Pause.*) All those people. Driving home. Look at that. (*Beat.*) I'd say, on balance, yes. You've got a much better view than us. In fact the whole neighborhood looks different from here. You've just got a much, much more pleasing view. (*Beat.*) By the way, why don't you ever ask me anything?

JOY. What like?

DALE. I don't know. Normally birds want chapter and verse. In two months. You haven't asked me a thing. I mean...

JOY. What's your favourite colour, Dale?

DALE. Right.

JOY. What's your favourite food, Dale?

DALE. Forget it.

JOY. If you could meet any famous person –

DALE. Forget it. Forget I said anything.

JOY. If you could come back as any animal –

DALE. What's the scariest thing you've ever done?

JOY. What's the scariest thing you've ever done? (*Pause.*) Come on. What's the scariest thing you've ever done?

Pause.

DALE. I once got my head stuck in a hole.

Pause.

JOY. What hole?

DALE. I was in the Cubs. On a sixers' camp out near North Mimms. We went looking for animal tracks. We were supposed to do plaster casts of deer prints. Badger prints. I went off on my own. Got my head stuck in a hole.

JOY. How?

DALE. I just followed these tracks. And they led to a hole. I thought I'd have a look in. See who was home. So stuck my head in. I was there for hours.

JOY. I can't bear it, Dale. What did you do?

DALE. I just waited. Waited for something to come along and tear my eyes out. Eat my little face. Pull out my tongue. I don't know. It was pitch dark.

JOY. Who found you?

DALE. The other Cubs. They got a spade and dug me out. I was eight.

JOY. What would you rather be eaten by, a shark or a lion?

DALE. Pass.

JOY. You can't pass.

DALE. A lion.

JOY. Why?

DALE. A lion is a professional. Holds you down and chokes you. You just drift off. Whereas your shark... he just keeps rushing up and taking great big bites. No one needs that.

She laughs.

If I'm going to get eaten I'd rather not be there when the actual eating part goes down. I'd rather be swiftly dispatched, then eaten. Finally, a lion shares you with its offspring. It's just more of a family occasion. Also, I've never been to Africa.

JOY. Why don't you want to be there? This is the last thing you're ever going to do, ever. There's nothing after it. I want to know what it's like to be ripped apart. To be devoured in two or three big bites. I want to be ripped limb from limb. I want to see my blood on the water. I want to be there. I want to feel it. To be devoured. Whole. Sudden. And in ten seconds, nothing. I'm gone.

DALE. What's the scariest thing you've ever done?

JOY. This.

Pause.

DALE. I better go.

JOY. She took her squash stuff. She's got squash.

DALE. Yeah but –

JOY. It's Lyn v Pauline. It's a fight to the death.

Pause.

DALE. After that first barbecue, I said to Lyn, she was brushing her teeth I said, 'Nice pair. Nice couple. He's a laugh. She don't say much. Just sits there and drinks a whole box of wine.' But Lyn weren't having it. She says to me, 'It's early days, Dale. She's shy. Trust me. That one just needs warming up.' (*Beat.*) Then the very next day, scorcher it was, I look out the window and there she is, next door, on a lounger, and she's in just a bikini. She's lying there in the all-together. And the funny thing is, as I'm looking down on her, out the window, the funny thing is, I could be wrong but it looks like she's looking straight back at me. And what if she doesn't sit up, pop her top off and lie there, in just her bikini bots. Gazing up at me. I was thinking, 'Lyn. I take it all back. I stand corrected. She's just shy. That one just needs warming up.' Did you see me, Joy?

JOY. I couldn't possibly say.

DALE. Like you're looking at me now.

JOY. Just like this.

DALE. Then you took it off.

JOY. How?

DALE. Show me.

JOY. How was it?

DALE. Show me. You slut.

JOY. Slut.

DALE. You dozy slut.

JOY. Dirty bitch.

DALE. You dirty whore. Show me.

The phone rings. Once. Twice. Three times. Four times.

NED (*on the answerphone*). Joy. Are you there? If you are
there, pick up. No? It's me. I'm in the Travelodge at
Cheshire Services. Had a successful day. The room isn't bad
actually. I've got my own tea-making facilities. And Sky
Sports. But you have to key in a code and I haven't got it.
Anyway, I've got two short meetings in the morning, and
then I'll hit the road. I should be back by bedtime… Well,
I'm going to get some sleep now. Well, sleep well. My little
cuddly toy. Night night, cuddly toy.

Silence.

JOY. If you could live anywhere in the world, where would it
be?

Pause.

DALE. What?

JOY. Somewhere warm? Somewhere far away, over water? You
know where I'd go? Anywhere it's spring. Early spring.
Warm sunlight and cool shade.

DALE. He thinks you're nicking his stuff. He does. He thinks
you're picking him clean.

JOY. Now why would I do that?

DALE. Why indeed? How did you get the birdbath out?
Seriously. How did you nick his birdbath?

JOY. Strictly speaking, that was my birdbath.

Silence.

DALE. Going somewhere?

JOY. What if I was?

Pause.

DALE. Going somewhere are we, Joy? Are we going somewhere?

Pause.

JOY. I don't know, Dale. Are we?

Blackout.

Spotlight on:

DALE (*pause*). You've lived for years in the one house. For years. You know which window sticks, which floorboard creaks. Which tap drips. The cold spots. The damp patch. You know it. Like the back of your hand. You could walk round it – blindfold. Fix a lightbulb. Make a cup of tea. In your sleep. Find your way – Upstairs. To bed. Blindfold. Then one day. One day, you're in the house. Fixing a bulb. Leaky tap. Damp patch. Cup of tea. And you look round and there's… There's – a door. There's a door there. A door you never saw before. In your house. Right there. Before you. A door. A new door. Was it always there? How could you not notice it. How could you not have seen it before? Would you open it?

Blackout.

Spotlight on NED. *Watching his old tapes. Explosions on his television. Louder and louder.*

Spotlight on:

I can't sleep. I wait till Lyn's dropped off, then I'm up, pacing. If she's working nights, I'm up the allotment. Sitting in the shed. Waiting. Watching. (*Pause.*) I'm in the car in a

layby. Watching the cars go by. In the car park of the
Arndale. I've started smoking. For something to fucking do.
Nine nights out of ten, nothing. Then on the tenth, there's her
car. Pulling into the car park. I get out, go over, but she's not
there. I can't see her anywhere. Joy? Joy?

Spotlight on JOY.

NED. Dale.

DALE. Jesus. Ned. You scared me.

NED. Is that you? What are you doing here? It's three o'clock.

DALE. Me? I couldn't sleep.

NED. Small world. (*Beat.*) I just thought I'd pop up here. Run
through my calculations. Dot the 'I's. You can't be too
careful. You've only got to overlook one tiny detail and you
end up with egg on your face.

Beat.

DALE. Well, I best be off. You coming?

NED. No, you go on. I'm going to hang about for a bit. You
know, it's funny. Looking at this old thing. I've always
thought she was a monstrosity. But right now, in the dark,
silent, she looks almost beautiful. It's always the same. Right
before the big day, right before the drop, they always look…
innocent. Pure. Like they're begging you not to do it.

DALE. Goodnight, mate.

NED. Give my best to Lyn.

DALE. I walk back to my car and I get in and I drive. I can see
him in the mirror, standing there in the dark, still, watching
me drive away. I drive home, pull in the garage and she's
there. On her front lawn.

JOY. That first barbecue. I thought you were a ghost. I thought
you were all ghosts. Ghouls. In the dark. Laughing. But
you're the one warm thing I've touched for years. The only
thing that's been there in years. I can barely look at you.

(Pause.) Come with me…

Spotlight on DALE.

DALE. Where?

JOY. Tonight. I'm leaving tonight.

DALE. Where are you going? *(Pause.)* Where are you going? What shall I bring?

JOY. Nothing. I've got money.

DALE. Where are you going?

JOY. Meet me in the car park of the Arndale at midnight. Don't bring anything. If you're not there, you'll have lost me. You'll have missed me. Will you be there?

Blackout on DALE.

JOY *turns.* NED *is there, on the couch. He doesn't turn to look at her.*

Ned. I thought you were out.

NED. I got cold. I came back.

JOY. I thought I'd go for a walk. I can't sleep.

NED. You want to watch telly? Or we could go to bed. Come to bed, we can have a cuddle.

JOY. I need some fresh air.

NED. It's cold out there. You sure you don't want to come to bed?

JOY. I shan't be long.

Pause.

NED. Well, it'll do you good. I'll tell you what. I'll wait up. I'll be here when you get back. I'll wait for you.

Pause.

JOY. Goodnight, Ned. Sleep well.

NED. Goodnight, my love.

He watches her leave. Music. Lights fade to black.

A surtitle appears:

'It started to rain.'

Spotlight on:

DALE. It was a combination of factors. First up, do the maths. It was one summer. Add it up… Once in the shed. Once in her car. Once in the woods. Once round hers. Four times. End of the day, the whole plan was half-baked. It was full of holes. Apart from the where, what and how, I've got the business to think of. I've got responsibilities there to thirty-odd blokes. Not to mention the kids. Did I mention the kids? Me and Lyn, we've got two. One of each. I'd die for those kids. They mean, they mean the absolute world to me. In any equation, they come first. So whatever it was, whatever combination of reasons, when it came to the crunch, I never showed up. I watched her leave her front door, and walk past our house, without looking up, to the end of the close. And there she stopped, at the dark end. There she stood. Still. Looking out up the main road. Just standing there, the cars whizzing by. You couldn't help but feel for her. She stood there for thirty minutes. An hour. Then she turned round, and walked back up the street, back to her house. And went inside. And closed the door. (*Beat.*) Me, I went down to the kitchen, to make Lyn a hot-water bottle, nice cup of hot chocolate. And I walked out in the garden, while the kettle · boiled. It had stopped raining. And there he was.

Lights up on NED, *looking at him.*

DALE. Ned?

NED *smiles.*

Ned, mate. Are you okay?

NED *just stares at him.*

Look, Ned... It was... Ned. Please.

NED. Help me, Dale. Help me. Please. You have to. Please help me.

DALE. What?

NED. Please. Please don't let me fall asleep. Don't let me fall asleep.

DALE. Ned –

NED. I don't know what I'll do. I... I... Please. I... I'm falling... I'm... Help me.

DALE. Ned –

NED. It's coming. It's coming for me. For me.

DALE. Oh my God.

NED. No. No. No. Please. Help me.

DALE. And then he told me. He told me his dream.

Blackout. Pause.

Spotlight on:

NED. I'm alone. In the middle of a forest. I'm surrounded by tall pines. It's freezing cold. I feel the wind. The dry, dry wind. On my face. The awful dry chill. Suddenly I see walls growing up around me. Brick by brick. Bricks growing all around. One on the other. Faster and faster. Four walls rising up. Wallpaper growing. Light switches. Fittings. Carpet growing beneath my feet.

A ceiling, closing overhead, closing out the light. I'm closed into a room. I'm in the middle of a room. I know the room.

It's a bedroom. My bedroom. (*Beat.*) I'm home. I turn
around. And I see it. I see it all. Everything. Everything I'd
lost. Everything. It was all there.

Music. Lights up slowly as NED *turns around. The lights
come up on all of the things he has lost. The room is full of
clocks. Golf clubs. Stuffed badgers. Busts. Books. Lawn-
mowers. The tandem. The beekeeping kit. The birdbath.
Everything. From out of the birdbath, he picks up the gold
cufflinks. Holds them up to the light. Reads the inscription.
He puts them back.*

*The light catches the bed. A figure lies covered there,
sleeping.*

*He walks over. And stands watching her sleep. Slowly he
picks up the cricket bat. He holds it in his hands. He slowly
raises it and brings it crashing down on the sleeper. Over
and over.*

Blackout.

Instant spotlight on:

JOY. I stand at the end of the street. I close my eyes and listen
to the sound of the rain and the cars whizzing by. Soon the
sounds fade. There's nothing but darkness. And when I open
my eyes, the cars have gone. The road has gone. The houses
have gone. I'm standing in a forest. After rain. I take a step
forward. Another. I don't turn round. I just walk. Away. I
don't look back. The wind whips up. I'm running against the
wind and it's pushing me back. And suddenly the wind
changes and it's behind me, pushing me along, carrying me
further and further away. And I close my eyes. And I run.

Lights fade to black.

Spotlight on:

DALE. It's funny. You live six feet apart and your paths never seem to cross. Take the couple on the other side. The Harrisons. Pam and Phil. Pam and Pete. Paul. Honestly, they've lived there five years I couldn't pick him out of a line-up. Not like the other side. You'll not be surprised to hear we're still thick as thieves. Still in each other's pockets. The ladies went for a pint only last week. And I bumped into Ned on his way to work this morning. Chatted about this and that. Pencilled in a barbecue. But we never talked about that night. The night he told me his dream. (*Beat.*) Before he rushed off, I asked him if it was still happening. If his stuff was still going missing. 'You know me, Dale. I've got that much junk. That much rubbish I can't keep track of it. I'd lose my head if it wasn't screwed on. What it needs is a good spring clean.' (*Pause.*) They blew up the Arndale Centre Tuesday. Drew a crowd of over a thousand. There was hot dogs, a brass band, kids dancing with their dads and everything. The press was there. The local TV news. I bumped into Ned, but he was too busy to talk. Had this hard hat on. And a walkie-talkie. And now I think of it, yes, unless I'm mistaken, he did look better. Thinner. Less tired. Mind you, it was dark. (*Pause.*) She was there too. Joy. Standing a few rows behind us, among the crowd, in her black mac, shivering, looking up into the dark. (*Beat.*) Then suddenly, a hush fell over the crowd, there was a drum roll, and everyone joined in together, all the mums and dads, all the families what had shopped there for years, all chanting together ten, nine, eight, seven… SIX, FIVE, FOUR, THREE, TWO, ONE – and there was this rumble and the whole thing came crashing down, and when the smoke cleared there was just dust and rubble for ever. Then suddenly, the skies opened and it started to rain.

DALE *looks up.* NED *and* JOY *appear in the half-light, standing apart, still, gazing up at the dark sky.*

The End.